Quilts and Country Gardens
Remembering a Simpler Time

by Marilyn Kratz
Illustrated by Beverly Behrens

Happy Memories!

Marilyn Kratz

prairie hearth
publishing, llc

ISBN 978-0-692-46983-5

Text copyright © 2015 by Marilyn Kratz
Illustrations copyright © 2015 by Beverly Behrens

Cover illustration, quilt blocks, and botanical prints by Beverly Behrens
Cover Design by Melanie Bender

Copyedited by Kathy K. Grow, www.DoWriteEditing.com

First printing August 2015

Published by:
Prairie Hearth Publishing, LLC
PO Box 569
Yankton, SD 57078

Dedication

I dedicate this book to my husband, Bud (Ernest), and his siblings, pictured below. They took me into their family almost sixty years ago and made me feel it was also mine.
MK

Pictured left to right – Marsha Kratz Beran, Kay Kratz Schoenfish, Ernest (Bud) Kratz, Coletta Kratz Bender

I dedicate this book to the lively memories of childhood visits with my Great Aunt Effie at her South Dakota farm. I remember the flower garden — and its gate where I'd swing. And I recall quiet afternoons looking on as Aunt Effie worked her beautiful Flower Garden quilt. That quilt is now among my treasures, adding its soft beauty and special warmth to my home.
BB

Introduction

Remembering the simpler times in which we grew up is sort of like snuggling under a quilt made by someone we love. Those memories have a way of warming us as nothing else can. Perhaps the days weren't all that easy when we lived them long ago; maybe we remember mostly the good parts. But that's just fine. I hope these stories bring back your happiest memories.

TABLE OF CONTENTS

Flower Basket Quilt Block

Quilts: A Labor of Love

My mom made the quilt I take out each spring after it's too warm for our wool blanket. Sometimes, as I relax under that old quilt, I think about all the work that went into it and all the others she created so many years ago.

The first step was constructing the decorative top. Sometimes she used a pretty colored sheet for the top; that saved a lot of work. But often, Mama spent many winter evenings sewing small pieces of fabric into a pattern. Sometimes she ordered them precut from a catalog. While that also saved a lot of work, it still took hours of fancy stitching to sew the pieces to each block of the quilt. After the blocks were completed, Mama sewed them together with her treadle sewing machine.

Before the top could be joined to the quilt's middle and bottom layers, the stitching pattern had to be determined. On pieced quilts, one often followed the edges of the pieces, or, if the quilt top was one Mama had ordered from a catalog, the stitching lines were printed on it.

On quilts made with patterned sheets, the pattern could guide the stitching. On solid-colored sheets, Mama had to put a pattern on it. She used a cardboard stencil to do that, tracing the pattern over and over with an ordinary lead pencil until it covered the entire quilt top. Most pieced quilts had a solid-colored border around them, so that had to have a stitching pattern traced on it, too.

The underside of the quilt might be a bedsheet or cotton fabric, cut to size. She often chose a pretty color or pattern for that, too, so the quilt could be reversible.

1

Then Mama was ready to set up the quilt frame. This consisted of four long, narrow boards and four corner stands with clamps. The long boards were clamped in place at each corner on top of the stands to form a square. A strip of heavy cotton cloth was nailed to the inside edges of the four boards.

Mama pinned the underside fabric of the quilt to the frame's cloth strip all around the edges. Next she spread a thin layer of cotton batting over it. Then she laid the quilt top over that and pinned the three layers together. Finally, Mama hand-sewed the edges of all three layers to the strip of fabric attached to the long boards, and the quilt was ready for quilting.

After the quilt had been quilted about a foot or so in from each side, the corner clamps were released so the quilt could be rolled onto the long boards. That put an unquilted area within reach of the quilters, who sat on all four sides to work.

Mama invited neighbor ladies and relatives to come help with the quilting. Of course, the ladies came with their husbands and children, and they'd expect a generous "lunch" at the close of the evening. So Mama's next "quilting" tasks were baking a big cake, making lots of chicken salad or ham sandwiches, and putting a few jars of home-canned peaches in the refrigerator to chill.

Quilting bees were like a party to us when we were children. We'd have other children to play with, and then there'd be a good lunch before they went home. I'm sure Mama was exhausted by the time the evening was over.

I learned to quilt as a young girl. My arthritic fingers no longer allow for such fine work, but I loved doing it years ago. I'm sure even Mama enjoyed it, too, once all the preparations were completed. After all, the actual quilting gave her a chance to sit and rest her feet while only her fingers worked.

Snapdragons

Morning Glory quilt made for author by her mother

The Morning Glory Quilt

When winter's frigid nights finally fade
And spring brings gentle welcome warmth,
I gladly pack away my heavy woolen blanket
And spread a bouquet of morning glories across my bed.

Mama made the quilt for me, appliqueing with tiny stitches,
The brilliant blue blossoms, centered with sunny yellow,
And vines and leaves in two shades of green
On the white background.

As I softly brush my hand across the stitches,
I feel the love in every square she created.
I picture her in her rocker,
Working meticulously, patiently, hour after hour.

Did she dream of the day she'd see it
Spread proudly over the bed in my home?
Did Mama know how much I would treasure
Her gift of time and love?

Hydrangea

Payback Visits

When I was a little girl, people enjoyed visiting friends and relatives on Sunday evenings. And they didn't sit around watching television. They actually talked to each other.

At my home, this usually started with my parents discussing who had visited us lately. We then owed them a visit. It was expected that the visit had to be returned after a suitable length of time.

Mama would phone the family we intended to visit to check if they'd be at home. The phone call had another purpose, too. Mama knew the lady of that house would want to know ahead of time that someone was coming so she could get something ready to eat at the close of the visit.

I'm sure it wasn't always easy for women to come up with a late-evening "lunch." Living out in the country, as most of our friends and relatives did, they had to make do with whatever they had on hand. One lunch we were sometimes served consisted of graham crackers broken up in sauce dishes and topped with canned peach halves and whipped cream—real whipped cream, since most people we visited milked cows. There was certainly no reason to complain about that simple, yet sweet and delicious, dessert.

I remember one evening when we visited my great-aunt and great-uncle in town. My great-aunt must not have had anything baked to serve us because she set out cheese and crackers. It was the first time I'd ever eaten that combination, and I thought it was delicious and almost exotic.

If someone called to tell us they were coming to visit, Mama would hustle to bake a cake, if the call came early enough, and send one of us children down to the cellar to get a jar of home-canned fruit. Sometimes, she'd quickly grind up some cooked chicken and make sandwiches. Then she'd need a jar of homemade pickles from the cellar, too.

Sunday night visits were the most common, although, in less busy times of the year, people visited on weeknights, too. All these visits usually began about seven o'clock and lasted until ten or eleven.

I especially enjoyed visits with families who had children to play with. While the grown-ups sat around in parlors and talked, we children always found plenty to do. Sometimes, when we planned to visit where there were no children, I'd beg my parents to phone my best friend's parents and ask them to visit the same people so I'd have someone to play with.

Visiting in the old days wasn't just for catching up with news, although that did happen. It provided entertainment and companionship before television isolated us in our homes.

Nowadays, when so much communication is done electronically, a good face-to-face visit would be a nice change. And having "lunch" together at the end would just be the frosting on the cake—or the whipped cream on the graham crackers and peaches.

Washing the Separator

My sisters and I always tried to be legitimately busy doing something else when it was time to wash the separator. We all hated that time-consuming job.

The separator was a machine which separated whole milk into cream and skim milk. The sturdy metal contraption, usually standing in a building away from the barn, had a large metal bowl on top into which Daddy poured milk, fresh from the cows.

Then someone had to turn the hand crank on one side, making the inside of the machine spin milk rapidly through small metal disks. Because skim milk is heavier than cream, it was pulled towards the outside of the separator's cylinder walls while cream collected near the middle.

Skim milk and cream emerged from separate spouts and emptied into pails. A small pail for cream sat on a round platform extending from one side of the machine. Skim milk poured into a big pail sitting on the floor.

We used skim milk to feed animals on the farm. Cream was transferred into a big can and sold each Saturday. Mama also kept a good supply of cream in the refrigerator for us to enjoy. I suppose she kept some whole milk on hand, too, although neither my siblings nor I enjoyed drinking milk.

It was important to keep the separator very clean. So, after the evening separating, Daddy ran a bucket of clean cold water through the machine to rinse it thoroughly. But that was not enough. After the morning use, the machine had to be taken apart and washed—piece by piece—and, believe me, there were a lot of pieces.

We'd start by lugging a big bucket of very hot water down from the kitchen to the separator house. First we'd wash the big pieces, such as the bowl and spout mechanisms. But then we faced the worst part of the job: the soup-bowl-sized disks. There were over twenty of them, and each had to be washed one at a time. Every bit of clotted cream had to be removed.

Sometimes, as I worked at this, I'd make up songs. I still remember every word of one I made up on a rainy day. It's a sad love song, and, yes, it's about rain. But I'll never ever sing it for anyone. It's too silly.

I was amazed recently to discover cream separators are still being made and sold. I suppose some people prefer doing things the hard way, but I'm glad I can buy my milk and cream in neat little cartons in the store—and not have to wash that big old separator.

Home Perms: Which Twin Had the Toni?

Hairstyles often featured curls when I was a girl. And to have curls in straight hair required getting permanent waves at a hair salon in town. The process took at least two hours and was usually scheduled on a Saturday evening because we'd be in town anyway. I didn't get to see a movie that evening or spend much time with my friends.

I was happy when home perms finally became available. I remember commercials about one brand called "Toni Home Permanent." They'd show a set of twins, one of whom supposedly had had a professional perm from a beauty shop, and the other one who'd had a "Toni." Of course, you could never tell which one had the Toni because they looked alike. That was supposed to make us believe we could achieve professional results by giving ourselves a perm at home.

And a lot of us did just that since it was so much less expensive than a salon perm. I started getting home perms when I decided wearing braids was too childish for me. I suppose I was about twelve.

I prevailed upon my older sister to put the perm in my hair, as it was quite a process. It started with wrapping my hair on plastic curler rods, using a piece of paper that looked like that with which people rolled their own cigarettes, to keep the hair from slipping off the curlers. Tiny rods made for tightly curled hair; larger rods made hair wavy.

Next my sister applied the perm solution, a strong-smelling liquid that came as part of the perm kit. One had to be very careful not to let that solution drip on furniture, clothing, or into our eyes. We used bath towels to try to keep if off our skin as best we could.

I had to sit with that smelly solution on my uncovered head for about half an hour. When the time was almost up, we had to unroll a curl and see if the waves in it seemed springy. If not, I sat and waited a while longer.

When it looked as though the perm had "taken," we had to rinse out the solution with lots of warm water. The last step was to apply another solution called "neutralizer." Only then could we unwrap my hair from the curlers. I may have forgotten a step or two, but that's about how it went, and it took an entire evening.

Perms kept our hair curly for about three months or until we got a haircut. Most women rolled their permed hair up in pin curls to achieve the style they wanted.

I remember a time when the style was to get a perm and then wear it frizzy, without using pin curls to tame it a bit. I did that for a few years. It was so easy; just get a perm, and from then on, my hair was "wash and wear."

My cousin Joan was about four or five when her mom gave her a home perm the first time, and then put her hair up in pin curls, let them dry, and combed them out. Apparently Joan didn't like her new look because, while her mom was out doing chores, she took a scissors and cut off all her curls. "Mom was not happy," Joan remembers, "but I look at the pictures Mom took, and I think the after-haircut picture looks better!"

Nowadays, when straight hair is in style, I doubt many people still get perms, and, if they do, they mostly have them done in beauty salons. I'm sure the results are fine, but I rather miss seeing the twins in those old commercials and wondering, "Which twin had the Toni?"

Petunias

Kerosene lamp used in author's childhood home

Lighting Up the Past

It's great to flick a switch and have light flood every corner of a room. I imagine most of us never give that convenience a second thought. But I remember the days, growing up on the farm, before we had electric lights to brighten up long winter evenings.

Back then, we depended upon kerosene lamps. They had a base that held a small tank of fuel. A cotton wick extended from the kerosene through a metal section and up into the glass chimney above it. The higher you turned up the wick by adjusting a knob at the side of the lamp, the higher and brighter the flame. Of course, if you turned it too high, you ended up with too much flame and a soot-coated lamp chimney.

We had a small lamp for each of the two upstairs bedrooms. I suspect they were the cheapest variety made since they were clear glass without fancy designs. The light they cast never reached into the corners of those rooms, but they certainly cast spooky shadows as the flame flickered inside the glass chimney.

For the kitchen, Mama had a fancier lamp somewhat larger than the ones used in the bedrooms. Its base was shiny metal. A cutout design decorated the bottom of the base.

I often sat at the kitchen table and looked at my reflection in the curved surface of the base. It acted somewhat like a mirror in a fun house, distorting my image into fantastic shapes. That may sound like a silly way to pass time, but those were the days before we sat watching TV for hours.

Our prettiest and biggest lamp sat on the dining room table and was used only when we had company. Its base was made of pressed green glass, much fancier than the clear glass of our bedroom lamps. Instead of a plain, flat wick, it had a circular type called a mantle, made of a delicate substance that would incandesce when heated by the flame. Surrounding the tall glass chimney was a shade of white glass with a clear-glass rim in a beaded pattern along the bottom. The shade rested on three thick wires extending from the center of the lamp.

Every Saturday morning, Mama washed all the lamp chimneys in hot sudsy water. She rinsed them in the warm-water well on one end of the cookstove before polishing them. That was one chore she hardly ever asked us to help with. I'm sure she preferred doing it herself to spending money to replace lamp chimneys broken by our fumbling hands.

When my parents moved to town, years after electricity had come to the farm, I asked Mama for her beautiful green glass lamp. It now sits on top of my hutch as a silent reminder of happy days gone by. In its own way, it still brings light to my life.

Spring on the Farm: A Busy Time

Spring on the farm meant different things to different members of my family. For my father, it meant many cold nights in the hog shed, making sure all the piglets being born survived. Sometimes he'd bring a tiny weak runt into the house to be nursed back to health by us children. We loved caring for those soft, clean babies with stiff hairs all over their bodies, but we steered clear of them when they grew into big, muddy hogs.

Daddy also had to be sure the cows made it through calving season all right, and that meant more nighttime trips out into the cold. Sometimes he'd have to pull a calf, and that could take a long time and was a lot of work. I'm sure he preferred the spring job of planting crops to helping birth animals, but both jobs were part of farming, and he loved his farm.

For Mama, spring meant baby chicks arriving from the hatchery in big, square, cardboard boxes with holes all around. I loved those fuzzy little balls of yellow fluff, but I hated the big old mean roosters they grew into. I didn't like hens either because they pecked at my hands when I gathered eggs.

Spring meant especially busy days for Mama as she spent every spare minute at her old treadle sewing machine, making new clothes to replace those we'd outgrown from last year. That included new sunbonnets, if we'd worn out those from the summer before. It was a good thing we had lots of baby animals to feed because she needed many printed feed sacks for all that sewing! She'd also spend days doing spring cleaning. She expected my sisters and me to help with that.

For my siblings and me, spring meant melting snow. We loved it when the ditches were full of water. When it finally got warm enough, we'd go wading amongst waterweeds as minnows nibbled at our toes.

We also loved gathering "seashells." Of course, they were really snail shells, most of them still harboring the animals that made them. Many a time, Mama scolded us for stuffing our pockets full of our little "seashells"—which she'd find when getting ready to toss our clothing into the washing machine.

I remember one spring activity that never seemed to work for me, and that was kite flying. We hardly ever had "store-bought" kites, but we often made them ourselves using thin branches and paper bags. To tell the truth, they were more fun to make than to fly because we could never get them to go high up into the air as they did in pictures we'd seen in books.

I always looked forward to the feeling of freedom inspired by shucking heavy coats, overshoes, and big flannel scarves as spring warmed the days. Soon Mama would insist we wear our sunbonnets and long-sleeved shirts to play outdoors in the scorching summer sun. But, for a few weeks between heavy coat and sunbonnet weather, we'd be free to run around outdoors with our heads uncovered and our winter-weary skin soaking up the warmth of spring sunshine. For us children, spring clearly meant fun.

Phlox

Windmill Blades Quilt Block

Revisiting the Farmyard

Even though it's been over fifty years since I lived on my parents' farm, I can still visualize many of the outbuildings. Maybe that's because, as children, my siblings and I found them great places to play and have adventures.

The big barn was one of our favorites. We loved playing in the haymow. Often we'd find tiny newborn kittens hidden up there by a mother cat. It didn't take us long to tame them.

The cats loved the barn, too. I'm sure it was because that's where they ate. Once in a while, we squirted milk into their mouths while we milked the cows. But mostly we fed them by pouring warm, fresh milk into a curious little black bowl, shaped somewhat like a shallow angel food cake pan, and made of a hard substance that might have been stone. I've often wondered where it came from and why it had that shape.

My younger sister and I got into trouble with Daddy one day when we were in the barn. We saw the horses' fly nets hanging in a small side room. They consisted of lots of thin leather strands which, when draped over a horse's back, would move and chase flies away. We decided to braid all those leather strands. When Daddy saw what we'd done, we were put right to work unbraiding!

The building Daddy called his shop was actually halfway underground. The top half was made of stones. Daddy had a forge in one corner of that building. I remember the excitement of watching him heat iron rods red-hot and then pound them into the shape he needed.

Daddy stored most of his tools, as well as his tractor, in the shop. Along one wall, he had hung a set of small boxes to hold various items. He said the boxes had come from the post office in a tiny town named Blaha which used to exist about a half mile from our farm. I've been told they'd be worth a lot of money now to antique dealers. I wonder if they're still there.

I didn't like the big hen house because I hated gathering eggs. Those hens didn't give up their treasure without trying to peck at my hand as I reached under them. I didn't tell Mama that I often took a stick with me when it was my turn to gather eggs. I'd use it to shove the hens' heads to the back of the nest while I took out the eggs. I suspect we had a few hens with bruised necks.

The little chicken coops near the big hen house were much more fun. I loved them when they were filled with downy little chicks. But they were even more fun when the chicks were big enough to be moved out. Then my sisters and I would clean the coops thoroughly and use them as playhouses.

Most of those buildings no longer exist. But I still enjoy wandering through them in my memories.

Rural School Memories

The rural school I attended many years ago stood in a big square playground surrounded by cornfields and alfalfa meadows. One teacher taught all grades, first through eighth. Most grades had only two or three students. I had the same classmate all eight years in grade school. She and I were best friends.

Each school day started with the flag pledge. On nice days, we recited it while standing around the flagpole in the schoolyard after some of the older children had raised the flag to the top. In winter, we stayed inside and faced a small flag posted in one corner of the room.

Then the teacher called one grade at a time to the "recitation bench" beside her desk. She'd check our work, explain the new lesson, and dismiss us to go back to our desks and do our new assignment, all in less than ten minutes per grade.

We looked forward to recess even though we had little playground equipment. Mostly, we enjoyed games such as Woods in the Jar, Lose Your Supper, tag, and baseball.

On cold or rainy days, we played inside. One of my favorite indoor games was "7-Up." To play it, seven people were chosen to be at the front of the room. The rest of us put our heads down and our thumbs up. The chosen seven tiptoed around the room and each touched one thumb. Then they called "Heads up," and those whose thumb had been touched tried to guess who had touched it. If they guessed correctly, they replaced the person at front.

I didn't realize until I was a teacher how wonderful this game was when students had to stay in at recess time. It was a very quiet game!

At noon we ate lunches we had brought in our "dinner pails." Our lunches consisted of sandwiches (made with homemade bread), fresh or canned fruit, and, if we were lucky, a sweet for dessert. My favorite dessert was a fresh pear, especially if I had a piece of Mama's delicious sour cream chocolate cake to go with it.

Our drinking water came from a rain-fed cistern in the schoolyard. We took turns pumping water from it to fill the small crock sitting on a bench in the schoolroom. We filled our cups, brought from home, using a dipper.

A huge coal furnace in the basement heated our school building in winter. The teacher kept it going by shoveling coal into it each recess. She "banked" it by adding an extra big amount of coal at the end of the day. It would burn slowly all night, making it easy to get the fire blazing again in the morning. Heat rose through a large metal grate in the floor above it. We stood on the grate and warmed our toes on cold days.

On a spring Sunday, just before the last day of the school term, everyone in the neighborhood gathered at school for a potluck picnic. Our moms set kettles of fried chicken, bowls of salads, and desserts of every kind on the teacher's desk and the library table. After the feast, we played games. One of the school board members made a quick trip into town and brought back a big cardboard bucket of ice cream in the afternoon to top off the picnic. How we looked forward to that treat. And how disappointed we were during the hard years after World War II when ice cream was not available, and we were served tart orange sherbet.

When I grew up, I decided to become a teacher. I was just nineteen years old, with one year of college training, when I started my first teaching position in a country school with thirteen students. I felt excited and nervous and happy as I prepared my lunch bucket the first morning of the term. I can't remember what kind of sandwiches I packed, but I do remember I put in a fresh pear and a piece of chocolate cake for dessert!

The Phonics Chart

It hung in a place of prominence at the front of the room. Every time you looked up from your desktop, you saw it—the dreaded phonics chart!

Oh, the hours we little students spent, sitting on a bench in front of that boring chart, going over each sound on the page. We started at the left with, for example, c. Then ca. Then cat. The next line might build the word mat. Then rat or hat or bat or fat.

I can see that chart in my mind's eye today as clearly as I saw the real thing over sixty years ago in the small one-room rural school I attended. I can even remember how it smelled—sort of old and musty.

The big black letters were printed on sturdy sheets of cream-colored paper about three feet square. Tattered edges showed years of hard use. Here and there, a strip of yellowing Scotch tape repaired a rip.

A seam across the middle allowed the chart to be folded in half for storage, but I don't remember the teacher ever taking it down from its place just to one side of the blackboards spanning the front wall of the room.

As we progressed from first to third grade (no kindergarten for us in those days), we moved to increasingly more complicated phonetic elements on the pages of the chart. And that was how we learned to read. Phonics also helped us learn to spell. We had no computers with spell check in those days, of course.

If you had asked me what I liked least about school when I was in any of the first three grades, I'm sure I would have answered, "Sitting in front of the phonics chart." It seemed so tedious to practice those sounds over and over.

Sometimes we sat there and did them silently. At other times, the teacher stood beside the chart and pointed to the letters with a long stick, and we'd all say them aloud together. She must have been as bored as we were.

But now I realize just what a wonderful foundation those hours gave me for reading and spelling skills. And, when I became a teacher, I still taught phonics, even when phases of reading instruction veered away from that basic method I learned as a child, sitting in front of the big phonics chart.

Sunflower

Cats lined up on barn doorsill on author's farm home

Farm Pets

Every child who grows up on a farm knows the difference between a farm animal and a pet. That didn't stop my siblings and me from trying to make pets out of most of the animals on the farm where we grew up. Often, it didn't work!

I had a special fondness for baby chicks. I couldn't resist those little cheeping balls of fluff. I was fascinated by the brooder house full of tiny black eyes in a sea of yellow. When Mama sent me to feed the chicks, I'd wait till they were comfortable with me standing in their midst. Then I'd clap loudly—once—to see all those black-dot eyes go down at the same time as the chicks reacted to the unexpected sound. I don't think Mama would have approved, but I thought it was great fun.

Chickens don't make good pets as a rule, but I remember a particularly friendly little rooster we named Oogie. We could get him to perch on our shoulders or follow us about. I suspect he grew up into one of those mean roosters that loved to chase me.

Of course, we had plenty of cats. Those that survived annual bouts of distemper made great pets, while keeping the farm's rodent population under control. We loved dressing kittens in doll clothes, but we had a terrible time trying to get them to stay in the doll buggy. Even Mama had her favorite cats, a tiger-striped gray and a solid black. They whiled away many a cold winter day snoozing under the cookstove.

Daddy usually kept a couple of dogs on the farm. He trained them to herd the cows home from the pasture at milking time. Each dog had its special place in our affections. I can still remember most of their names—Sport, Beauty, Spike—and Daddy's special favorite, a huge tan and brown dog he called Maddo. Those dogs were good playmates and loyal friends.

Once in a while, we'd tame a bucket-fed calf or befriend a little runt piglet that needed to spend a few days in a box beside the stove in order to survive. They were pets only while they were small. We kept our distance from Daddy's big workhorses, Dolly and Bill.

Eventually, we did have one animal that was just a pet. That fat little black pony named Bertie had no practical use whatsoever. The only way we could get a ride on her was to push, pull, or somehow lure her up near the house. Then one of us would jump quickly onto her back and hang on as she galloped to the barn where she preferred to spend her days eating and sleeping.

Many of my happiest childhood memories involve hours of contentment spent playing with animals. I learned much from them about love and responsibility. But they also taught me the importance of just having fun.

Pansies

Crown of Thorns Quilt Block

Celebrating Easter

When I was a girl, Easter was a three-day event. It started on Good Friday—a day we had off from school—and didn't end until after dinner on Sunday.

Nowadays, we almost seem to have forgotten to observe Good Friday. The church to which I belong usually has a service, but it's not as popular as the big one on Easter Sunday morning. I suspect many churches don't even have an observance of Good Friday.

But, when I was a girl, Good Friday was a big day. Most of the churches in my hometown of Scotland, in southeast South Dakota, participated in a three-hour-long service in City Hall. It lasted from twelve noon to three o'clock and concentrated on the last seven sentences Jesus was supposed to have spoken from the cross.

Each participating church was responsible for about fifteen minutes of the service. People could attend as many segments as they wanted to. The Good Friday story was told with scripture readings, short sermons, and some hymns.

We children liked to sit in the balcony during the services. That made it easier for us to come and go as we wanted, and to get by with a bit more whispering than we probably should have. I suppose some older people stayed for the entire three hours, but I doubt I ever did.

Good Friday was the day we were allowed to wear our new Easter outfits for the first time, usually a new dress and hat. (And we always wore gloves to match.) Hats were such an important part of our Easter outfits back then. Even as a young married woman, I continued the tradition of buying myself a new hat each Easter.

I remember particularly a hat I bought when I was a young teacher in Yankton. It had floppy orange silk flowers all over, and I bought a pair of elbow-length orange gloves (I still have them—wish I still had the hat!) to wear with it. I felt very elegant.

The next day, my pastor's son, who was one of my fifth-grade students, commented, "Boy, that was sure a funny hat you wore to church yesterday, Mrs. Kratz!" So much for glamor!

When my siblings and I were young, we always helped Mama dye Easter eggs on the Saturday between Good Friday and Easter Sunday. Then we'd go out and pull enough grass to fill a cardboard box to use as a nest for the eggs. I didn't really believe in the Easter bunny, but that was the purpose for the grass nest. I don't remember any Easters so snowy we couldn't make our Easter bunny nest of grass, either dried brown or fresh green.

Of course, the highlight of the entire weekend was Easter dinner at Grandma's house, where we had a big ham and plenty of decorated eggs to eat. It was a fitting way to top off a weekend of celebration ushering in spring.

Mama's Homemade Bread

Nothing brings back memories of my childhood home more than the aroma of freshly baked bread. Whenever I bake bread myself these days—using my bread machine to make dough easily—I remember seeing Mama stir up a huge batch of dough by hand.

Mama baked several loaves of bread at a time so she wouldn't have to bake so often for our family of six. Sometimes she used part of the dough to make one of the delicious German meals we loved. My favorite was bread dough dumplings. The little lumps of dough cooked up moist and fluffy over a layer of potatoes crisping golden brown in lard at the bottom of Mama's black iron skillet.

Baking bread years ago began with Mama taking the jar of yeast starter out of the refrigerator the night before baking day and setting it on the cupboard. The next day, after taking out enough starter to make the dough rise, she'd add a little more flour and water to the jar before putting it back in the refrigerator until the next baking.

She also sliced up a potato or two the night before, placed them in a heavy saucepan, covered them with water, and put the lid on it. She set the pan on the grate over the burners of the gas refrigerator. By morning, the potatoes were soft enough to mix into the bread dough.

Mama always shaped the dough into balls and placed two balls in each rectangular bread pan. Several of my friends say their mothers did the same thing. None of us could come up with a reason for shaping loaves that way instead of into one long loaf.

Mama pulled the two round loaves apart before slicing them. I never liked to have the slice with the torn side. I preferred my slice from the middle of the loaf.

Nowadays, I love the end slice of bread with lots of chewy crust. But I guess we children balked at eating our crusts because I remember Mama saying, "Eat your crust so you'll have rosy cheeks."

Mama stored bread in a special drawer in our old metal cupboard. It had a metal lid we slid back after opening the drawer. I don't suppose it kept bread fresh very well. Maybe it's a good thing it didn't last long in our family.

I remember how much we appreciated plastic bags when they finally became available. Mama ordered a set from Wynn Speece, the Neighbor Lady, who sold them over radio station WNAX. The set of bags contained a really big one Mama used to store bread. We held the bags shut with clothespins. It was years before bags that zipped shut were invented.

Mama made only white bread. I ate many a thick piece of her delicious bread topped with homemade wild plum jam or chokecherry jelly. But my favorite way of eating it was toasted. And it had to be toasted in a specific way.

First, we'd let the cobs in the firebox of the old iron cookstove burn down to glowing embers. Then we'd spear a thick slice of bread on the long meat fork. We'd hold it over the embers until one side was toasted; then we'd turn it over to brown the other side. When it was all toasty, with maybe a few almost-burned crumbs, we'd saturate it with home-churned butter. Mmmm! Nothing ever tasted better.

I've often heard the saying, "Bread is the staff of life." To me, it's also the source of many wonderful memories from the past.

Sunbonnet Sue Quilt Block

Sunbonnet sewn for author by Florence Hauck,
Menno, South Dakota

I Wish I Had My Sunbonnet

I hated that sunbonnet when I was a girl. It felt like a helmet on sweltering summer days, but Mama insisted my sisters and I wear those contraptions from early morning till suppertime.

Only on summer evenings, as the sun made its way down in the west and the shelterbelt of fully leafed elms shaded the entire farmyard, were we allowed to run around outside bareheaded with our braids freely flopping.

It wasn't that Mama worried we'd someday end up with skin cancer. And she didn't even think about the fact that tanned skin wrinkles faster as we age. No, those matters didn't bother Mama. She had just one worry: freckles! Mama had lots of them herself, and she was determined her daughters would not.

So, every year, before the first sunny days of summer, Mama checked to see if we needed new sunbonnets. When we did, we chose the fabric we wanted from her scrap box. Often our bonnets used up two or three different scraps, making them unique and colorful.

Mama started by cutting two rectangles of fabric that would extend from the back of the head to about five inches beyond the face. She stitched tunnels in them and stuffed those tunnels with ribs of cardboard cut from old shoeboxes. I sometimes wonder where she found enough cardboard for all our bonnets since we certainly didn't get that many new shoes.

The cardboard-stiffened rectangle was held in shape around the face by sewing on more fabric to cover the back of the head, extending

39

down to the bottom of the neck and partway around towards the front.

Mama sewed on two ribbons to tie at the back to keep the bonnets from sliding ahead and two more to tie under our chins to keep the relentless prairie wind from blowing the bonnets off.

I suppose I appreciated my bonnet on days when my sisters and I worked for hours under sweltering skies stacking oat bundles into shocks. They also helped keep edges of cornstalk leaves from cutting into our faces as we walked the rows picking cockleburs. But those bonnets were stiff, hot, and stifling.

So why do I long for one now?

It has occurred to me, all these years later, as I garden with greasy sun block slathered all over my face and neck and an old cap with a big visor on my head, that a sunbonnet would be perfect to keep me sheltered from the sun as it did when I was a girl. I might even look a bit less like a scarecrow as I weed my flower beds.

Sunbonnets and mamas: treasures we don't fully appreciate until we don't have them any longer.

A Summer Treat

Summer seems a time for fun, no matter what age we are. But I especially remember that season when I was young. We'd play "house" for hours in the shade of shelterbelt trees. Sometimes we'd play "bakery" and whip up lots of mud pies and cakes.

I once asked my mom what she did in summer when she was a girl. It turns out she played house much the same as we did. Her mother made the dolls she played with, sewing body and head shapes from muslin, and embroidering yarn faces on them.

Mama and her sisters used old broken plates and cups and empty sardine cans for their "dishes," as my sisters and I did. And, like me, she remembered making lots of mud pies. My sisters and I were pretty good at decorating them with bits of grass and leaves.

Another thing we had in common was our love of ice cream as a summer treat. However, obtaining it was much different in her day compared to the time of my childhood.

For one thing, her family didn't have an ice cream freezer with a handy crank. They started with a five-gallon tub filled with ice and salt. The ice cream mixture was poured into an empty gallon syrup can with the lid replaced securely. Then they pushed the syrup can down into the tub of ice and, using the handle on the can, turned the pail back and forth half-turns.

Every once in a while, they had to remove the can, take off the lid, and scrape the frozen ice cream mixture off the sides of the can and into the middle. Then they'd replace the lid and repeat the turning

41

process. It must have taken a lot of time and muscle to enjoy ice cream those days. It's good she had lots of siblings.

The ice they used came from their icehouse, a building I remember seeing when I was a very little girl. It was originally the sod house my great-grandparents built when they homesteaded their farm. After they later built a wooden house for themselves, they dug out the floor of the sod house to a depth of five or six feet.

During winter, the men cut blocks of ice from ponds and stacked them in the sod house with thin straw layers between and a thick one over the top. Mama said they usually had ice until well into June.

I guess I'm glad I live in a day when ice cream is as handy as a trip to the store, summer or winter. But I wonder if we appreciate it now as much as my mom did when it came with a whole lot more work and, certainly, anticipation.

Summer Jobs Were Hard

Hot summer days bring back memories of two of the hardest jobs I had to do in my childhood on the farm.

One was pulling cockleburs. In those day, most farmers didn't spray to get rid of weeds in their cornfields. They pulled them by hand with the help of their children.

That would be an almost impossible job these days with corn planted so thickly in close rows. But, back then, corn was "checked" when it was planted so stalks grew the same distance apart in all directions, allowing the farmer to cultivate between rows.

When Daddy was ready to have us pick cockleburs, he would awaken us early so we'd be done by noon. We'd dress in jeans, long-sleeved shirts, and sturdy walking shoes. Daddy wore his straw hat. My brother wore a baseball cap. We girls donned our homemade sunbonnets. In those "costumes," we were ready to withstand heat from overhead, sharp-edged corn leaves at face level, and nasty sandburs on the ground.

Daddy assigned us each a row or two, and the walking began. We kept our eyes cast down, looking for pesky weeds to pull. If we found one too big to pull, Daddy chopped it off with a big corn knife which looked something like a saber.

Up and down the rows we walked until the field was weed free, and we were sweaty, dusty, and tired.

The other dreaded summer job was shocking oat bundles, and it was even worse than pulling cockleburs! Instead of walking in at least a little shade provided by tall cornstalks, we had to work in blazing July sunshine. And those oat bundles were heavy!

Usually, my older sister and I worked together. We'd start by setting two bundles against each other. Then we'd pile about six more bundles against them to make a shock. The shocks stood there, oat kernels safely drying out at the top, until threshing day.

The worst part of shocking was lifting a bundle and finding a snake under it. They were harmless garter snakes, but they scared me anyway.

The only good part about picking cockleburs and shocking oat bundles was getting the job done so we could go back to the house. Mama usually had icy cold watermelon waiting for us.

Picking cockleburs and oat shocking: two jobs I'd rather reminisce about than ever do again.

Potted Primroses

Cistern near corner of house on author's farm home

Cisterns: Water Source in Long-Ago Days

Most farms had cisterns when I was a girl. Instead of using water from a convenient faucet, supplied by a public utility, we had to go to the cistern to get water for household use.

To make a cistern, a hole about ten feet deep and six feet across was dug, usually on a high spot near the house. Cement applied to the sides and bottom of the hole kept dirt from falling into the water.

On top of the hole, a wooden or cement platform held a device for drawing up water. Sometimes it was a metal box-like structure with little tin "cups" on a chain going down into the water. It could be wound with a handle to draw up the filled cups.

However, on our farm, we had a big cylinder which I remember as being made of some type of pottery material. It had a tin top with a door in the center. We opened the door, dropped a pail attached to a rope down into the water, and hauled it up. No easy cups on a chain for us!

Usually, we used rainwater to fill the cistern. Daddy would wait a few minutes after the rain started to give it a chance to wash the roof. Then he'd turn a crank which opened the end of the downspout connected to the eaves trough and allowed water to flow into a metal box filled with charcoal. Water then drained through the charcoal and on into the cistern.

If we had a dry spell, Daddy would buy a tank of water when our supply ran low. Before pumping the water into the cistern, Daddy would clean the reservoir. He'd go down into it using a ladder and scrub the walls and floor. I remember seeing pails of muddy water being lifted out during the process.

Even with Daddy's efforts to clean the roof before catching rainwater and his scrubbing the cistern once in a while, I now often wonder how clean the water actually was. Surprisingly, we didn't have any problems with illness caused by our water. Maybe we were just more immune to germs in those days.

We children were cautioned to stay away from the cistern. However, when my parents weren't looking, my younger sister and I used to open the lid on top and shout down into it just to hear the echo. We ignored the danger of falling in, but my husband, Bud, knows that danger was real.

When he was just four years old, Bud and his five-year-old sister, Kay, were playing on top of the cistern beside their house. The wooden top gave way and Bud fell in.

Luckily, their cistern had a pump on top to draw up the water. Bud grabbed on to the pipe leading from the pump down into the water—a few feet above the actual water level—and held on while Kay ran for help.

One neighbor lowered another man into the cistern, holding on to the straps of his overalls, and the man pulled Bud up. He received only a bruise on his hip and a scratch on his arm, but I don't think Bud needed any more warnings to stay off the cistern.

I'd never give up the convenience of clean, running water coming out of a faucet, but I treasure the memories I have of cisterns. They were a unique and important part of growing up on a farm.

Cosmos

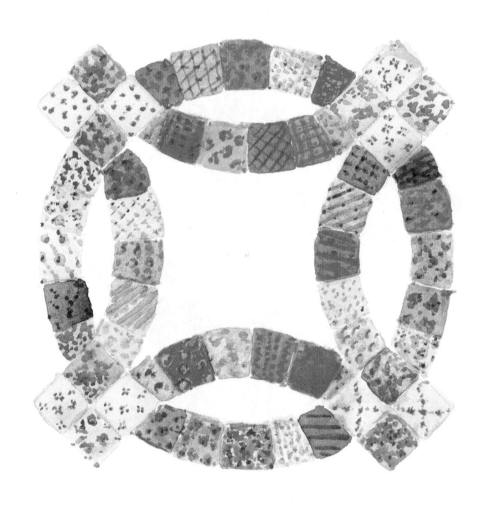

Wedding Ring Quilt Block

Wedding Traditions from the Past

I suppose we all think of weddings when June rolls around. I know I do, but maybe that's because I was a June bride myself many years ago. These days, brides take pride in inventing new touches for their special day, but I suspect they still rely on some of the old traditions. I don't get to attend many wedding these days, so I wonder how many of the traditions so familiar to me when I was young are still being honored.

For example, the flowers in most church weddings years ago were gladioli in the bride's chosen colors. Usually there were two tall white baskets of them at the front of the sanctuary. And the bride's bouquet often featured roses.

Wedding receptions years ago in our rural area were hardly ever held in a restaurant or events center as many are now. If the church basement was large enough, they would be there. If not, the bride's father rented a facility such as the city hall.

Since the reception was not held in a commercial eating establishment, family members provided refreshments at small gatherings, and the Ladies Aid of the bride's church prepared sit-down meals when large groups—maybe as many as three hundred—were expected. After a big hot meal and wedding cake, my dad handed out candy bars at our wedding.

At big receptions, the bride asked her friends to be table waitresses. She provided each waitress with an apron to wear while serving. Those aprons were usually sewed by the bride or her mother. They were mostly decorative, being made of netting or organdy in the bride's chosen colors.

The aprons served as thank-you gifts for the waitresses as well as a souvenir of the wedding. I remember I had quite a collection of them when I was young. At big weddings, we waitresses really earned our gift apron. Not only did we serve the food, we also helped clean up after the meal.

Nowadays, most people shop for wedding gifts from a list of items the bride and groom have registered at several stores and online. While that's a nice way of doing things, I think it takes a lot of fun out of opening gifts. There are few surprises.

Instead of having gifts delivered to the bride's home, as is often done these days, people used to bring their gifts to the reception. Sometimes the bride and groom opened them after the meal, holding each gift up high so everyone could see it. Or they had friends open them at the reception and display them on tables.

Of course, there always had to be one gag gift. Usually it was something silly to resemble a "chamber pot." I still have the little white enameled pot my husband and I received at our wedding. It makes a great container to hold paint when using a small brush.

I really miss the wedding write-ups they used to put in the local paper. Now they tell just time, place, and names of people involved. But, years ago, they always described the bride's gown and bouquet in minute detail. The colors worn by the bridesmaids and mothers of the couple were also included, as well as a description of the dress the bride wore to leave on the honeymoon.

I realize there are no absolutely right or wrong traditions to follow when planning a wedding. The marriage is, after all, the most important part. And that's one thing my husband and I got right, for sure!

A Time to Celebrate Freedom

If we didn't already realize what a great country we lived in, we had a vivid reminder of it every Fourth of July when we were children. Any time our parents took a day off—or even part of one—during the busy summer on the farm, it had to be for something important.

I remember how we hurried through our morning chores because we had to be in town by ten o'clock for the parade. Many churches and clubs made elaborate floats covered with paper napkins stuck into chicken wire forms on flatbeds pulled by pickups or cars. Those were the highlights of the parade. Area high school bands, antique cars, and prancing horses stretched the procession out for a good hour as we stood along the street and waved at people we knew passing by.

After the parade, we joined our aunts, uncles, and cousins at Grandma's house there in town for a noon picnic in her shady yard. The women provided hot dishes, salads, and luscious cakes. Grandma served her homemade root beer, cold and sparkling.

While the adults relaxed and visited, we children hurried through our dinners so we could run the four blocks back to Main Street to get our first view of the carnival which had set up there. We knew we'd have to wait till evening to have our rides, but at least we could get a taste of the excitement and color.

We had to spend most of the afternoon at home. Sometimes Dad did a few hours of fieldwork. Sometimes we all just rested. Then we'd do evening chores early and have a quick supper so we could get back into town for the rest of the day's fun.

The carnival held such fascination for us as children. We loved riding the merry-go-round with its elegant steeds. We floated high over the scene in the rocking seats of the Ferris wheel. If we were brave enough, we tried the wild and spinning "Tilt-A-Whirl" ride. We were careful to save some money for those special treats unique to the day: colorful ice pops, corn dogs (called Pronto Pups back then), clouds of pink cotton candy, and refreshingly cold bottles of pop.

Just as the sun began to cast long shadows, we walked the few blocks to the baseball diamond at the edge of town. While our parents enjoyed the game, we spent most of that time playing around behind the grandstand and begging for one more quarter to get one more treat. After the game, everyone settled in for the most important part of the day: fireworks.

The city fathers had set up the display at the far end of the baseball diamond. Everyone waited breathlessly for the first rockets to shoot up and fill the sky with big brilliant bursts of colored sparkles. "Oohs" and "aahs" accompanied each new display. It never lasted long enough for me, but it was the perfect end to a wonderful day.

As we piled back into the car for the quiet ride home, we didn't have to wonder what it had all been about. We knew we lived in the most wonderful country on earth, where we could celebrate being free in such a special way. That's what Fourth of July was all about way back then, and it still is today.

The Cellar: Our Storm Shelter

The day started with a relentless sun blazing down on the farm-yard. Humidity made doing chores miserable, even in the morning. Daddy kept an eye on the sky because he knew it was the kind of day that could brew up a storm in a hurry.

By late afternoon, banks of angry-looking black clouds began to bubble up in the west. The wind, which had scorched the crops and garden all day, died down. Leaves on trees hung motionless except for an occasional slight shiver that made them seem to dance. Birds stopped singing. The whole world seemed to be holding its breath.

Then the clouds turned an eerie green and a sudden cold wind swept across the yard. Daddy rushed about closing barn and shed doors.

"Get the flashlight," Mama shouted. And we all knew we were headed for the cellar. There we'd be safe from whatever the storm had in store for us.

Our cellar was one room dug partway into the ground near the northwest corner of the house. All that showed from the outside was a small, grass-covered hill with a door on the east side. A small window high on the west wall had been covered with dirt so no light was allowed to enter.

The day turned strangely dark as we hurried down crumbling cement steps to the shadowy, cool cellar with its intriguing smell of damp earth. Daddy latched the door on the inside. We huddled near the feeble light of the flashlight and listened.

55

I made sure not to stand near one of the cracks in the cement floor because sometimes a snake or lizard hid there. Around us, Mom's jars of canned fruits and vegetables reflected the light from the flashlight. In one corner, a few potatoes left from last year's crops lay in a small pile.

Soon we heard the patter of big raindrops on the wooden cellar door, set at a backward slant in the hill. That sound was followed by sharp pings that could only be hail. We all prayed a tornado was not hidden in the wild sounds of the storm.

Mama and Daddy didn't say much as the storm roared on above us. I felt safe, just because they were there.

We didn't have a portable radio back then, so we stayed in the cellar until the noise of the storm died down and a thin sliver of sunlight outlined the cellar door.

Then we all made our way back up the steps and out into the yard. Rain-freshened air greeted us. Birds had begun to sing again. Aside from leaves and small branches littering the yard, all was well.

That experience was repeated many times when I was a girl, though I don't remember a tornado ever hitting our farm. It didn't seem there were as many back then as we have now.

Sometimes strong wind flattened the golden heads of oats to the ground, or hail shredded cornstalks into ribbons. But Daddy didn't let things like that get him down. I've often wondered at his—and all farmers'—courage. They still work so hard getting the crops in, only to lose them sometimes in a few minutes of bad weather. But they take it in stride and always look forward to next year. How I admire them.

These days, when the storm siren blows, we head for the basement. But, somehow, it just doesn't feel as safe as that old cellar did. Maybe it's because Mama and Daddy aren't there with me. It's just another time when I really miss them—and that old cellar.

Daffodils

Peony Quilt Block

Mama's Country Garden

Mama planted a big garden every year. Did she do it because she loved gardening, as I do? I suspect her gardens were more labors of necessity than labors of love because gardening is a lot of work, and Mama always had plenty of other work.

For many years, Mama planted her garden next to the windmill near the big barn. I suppose she used water pumped by the windmill into the stock tanks to irrigate her garden when needed.

While many hobby gardeners plant flowers around or amidst their vegetables, Mama's gardens contained only plants that would produce food for our family. She planted the usual vegetables—tomatoes, green beans, cabbage, carrots, and such—to can for winter use.

Mama also planted lettuce and radishes to use all spring and into summer until that season's hot winds withered them. She planted peas for us to eat right there in the garden. We loved "unzipping" the fat pods and shoveling plump peas into our mouths when taking a break from hoeing.

We treated kohlrabi as an "eat in the garden" vegetable, too, even though it required a trip back to the house for a paring knife to remove the tough green skin before we could bite into the tangy, crisp, white flesh.

Mama didn't plant sweet corn in her garden. For many years, we ate field corn while the kernels were still plump and milky. In those days, most field corn my dad planted was not grown from hybrid seeds, so it was all right for us to eat it. When she finally did plant sweet corn, she did so at the edge of a cornfield. That's where she planted watermelons and cantaloupe, too. I can still remember how good those vine-ripened melons tasted on a hot summer day.

Each spring, we children helped Mama cut up potatoes left from the last year, being sure to have at least one "eye" on each piece. We planted row after row of them in a field behind the house. Daddy used his horses to plow the furrows open. We followed after, being sure to push the potato pieces in eye-side-up. In the fall, we had to go up and down those rows again to dig up the potatoes, using a special flat-bladed potato fork, and haul them in gunnysacks to the cellar. Potatoes were a lot of work at each end of the growing season!

When Daddy put up a fence around the house to keep chickens from messing on the front steps, Mama let me plant flowers in the fenced-in area. A lot of what I planted didn't survive. But I was able to raise such old-fashioned favorites as zinnias, marigolds, bachelor buttons, and four-o'clocks. I had a little luck with irises along the south side of the house.

I devoted about a fourth of the entire space to a big patch of moss roses. Those persistent little plants seeded themselves every year and filled the slope beside the cistern with a carpet of jewel-toned blossoms. I still grow them in my own garden and love them as much as I did back then.

The hobby of gardening seems to be growing in popularity these days. But, even though it was more of a necessity in my childhood, Mama took a lot of pride in her garden produce. Maybe that compensated for all the work it took to raise it.

Dangers on the Farm

Farming is a dangerous occupation. There are just so many big and powerful machines used to plant, maintain, harvest, and store crops. Each fall, I remember corn-picking accidents, perhaps because they happened to some people close to me.

One autumn morning when I was a little girl— in the days before corn was combined—my dad and his brothers were picking corn. They used a secondhand Bell City Single Row corn picker pulled by a tractor. Suddenly, my uncles rushed back to the farmhouse with my dad, whose hand was wrapped in a blood-soaked handkerchief. Mama rushed out of the house, followed by us children.

"He got his hand caught in the corn picker," one of the uncles said as Mama started crying. "Doesn't look too bad, but he'll have to have the doctor look at it."

Well, it turned out that Daddy had lost only the tip of one finger. For the rest of his life, that finger grew just a nubbin of a fingernail.

One of my uncles wasn't so lucky. He lost his entire hand in a corn picker and then had to wear a metal clamp on the end of his arm. He became very handy with it. He even had a special device to put in the clamp to hold his cards when playing pinochle.

Even milking could be hazardous. Some cows were kickers. We had a device of chains and clamps we could put on the back legs of particularly skittish cows while we were milking them. But sometimes even an old dependable cow would kick if a fly bit too hard. Then the pail of milk, the three-legged stool, and, usually, the milker, would go flying.

Daddy always warned us to be very careful with the long corn knives we used to chop particularly big sunflowers as we walked the cornfields. He didn't let us use them until we were old enough to do so correctly and safely.

Just playing around the farmyard could be dangerous. I remember "swimming" in the stock tanks when our parents left us alone on a hot summer afternoon. Or scrambling around on machinery when Daddy wasn't looking.

My most hated chore—"picking" eggs out of the nests in the hen house—often resulted in being pecked on the hand by hens that didn't want to give me their eggs. Even the roosters were a threat, chasing us and scratching at our legs with their sharp claws.

Because we grew up with all the potential dangers on the farm, maybe we learned almost automatically how to protect ourselves. I don't think we took chances with things that might have injured us. Or maybe we were just lucky most of the time.

Tomatoes

Author's father, wearing overalls, with her mother as they celebrate the first birthday of their eldest grandchild

Daddy Loved His Overalls

You don't see many men wearing overalls these days, not even farmers. They seem more comfortable in jeans and T-shirts. But I always picture my farmer dad in his overalls.

Daddy wore overalls every day of the week except Sunday. On that day, he dressed in a suit for church. All the men did. I think he usually wore a tie to church, too, although maybe he skipped that torture in summer. Daddy much preferred overalls. I remember hearing him say how comfortable they were because they were loose at the waist.

Daddy had pinstripe navy and white overalls and some just plain dark blue; both were made of sturdy denim. The seams were double-stitched, and the pockets had rivets at the ends of each opening to keep them from tearing out. I don't remember ever seeing an overall pocket rip out at the corners.

Those overalls were a marvel of storage spaces. Across the front bib were several little pockets. Some held pencil stubs; some were used for stray nails and bolts. The pockets at the waist were big and deep with a little key pocket inside the one on the right. Those big pockets held whatever tools Daddy might need for the job he was doing at the time. They also held big red or blue handkerchiefs with white and black designs on them. I don't remember what Daddy carried in his back pockets, but I'm sure he found uses for them, too.

Sewn into one side seam was a sturdy loop just perfect for carrying a hammer or other tool with a long handle. In those overalls, Daddy was ready for the hard work of farming.

All week long, with his overalls, Daddy wore long-sleeved blue chambray shirts or dress shirts that were no longer good enough for church. The shirts and overalls often sported patches Mama added to repair rips and keep them in service as long as possible.

Daddy saved one pair of overalls just for going to town on Saturday evening. Usually the "going to town" overalls were pinstripe ones, and he wore them with a clean white shirt. I'm sure he felt very dressed up. Daddy would join other men standing around on the street corner for a good visit. He fit right in because almost all of them wore overalls, too.

Even after Daddy and Mama retired and moved into town, he wore overalls a lot of the time. Of course, they stayed a lot cleaner and neater with only tasks around the house and yard to do. But he saved some of the older ones to go out and help my brother on the farm whenever he could.

I treasure my memories of Daddy in his overalls. He always looked happy in them, doing what he loved best to do—working on his beloved farm.

Cabbage

School House Quilt Block

Recess Fun in Rural School

It's fun to drive past schoolyards and see children out playing on colorful and interesting playground equipment. It makes me think back to recess times in rural school days when the most important piece of play equipment we had was a huge open field of grassy weeds, and we made the best of that.

In fall and spring, bigger boys and girls played softball with the meager equipment—a few bats and a ball or two—we had on hand. Littler children enjoyed picking wild flowers in the ditches to give "Teacher" and playing pretend games. Often we all played games together, such as Ante Ante Over, Pump-Pump-Pullaway, and various forms of tag.

One of my favorite outdoor games was Going to New Orleans, a kind of charades game with two teams. One team would decide on an action and give the other team the initials of the words in the action. Then they'd start to pantomime it. If and when the second team discovered what the action was, they'd shout it out and run across the center dividing line to tag as many on the other team as they could. Those tagged had to join their team. I remember one time when we were playing that game, and an older girl decided our team would act out "Pressing Papa's Pretty Purple Pants." The other team never did figure out what "PPPPP" stood for.

If all else failed, we spent a recess in fall or spring drowning gophers. The equipment we needed was a pail to carry water from the cistern and our baseball bats. Someone would pour water down a gopher hole until the gopher ran out. Then the boys with bats would try to kill it. I don't think we ever thought of it as something cruel to do. And, besides, we hardly ever got the little critters.

During winter, we looked forward to a good nighttime snow. Then we could play Fox and Goose the next day. We'd tramp out a big circle with lines radiating from it to the base at the center. We'd play that wonderful tag game until the paths were so obscured from running around that we had to quit and wait for fresh snow.

Sometimes we scratched out Hopscotch grids in the gravel of the short driveway into the schoolyard. We used small rocks to play the game.

I loved playing the circle game Lose Your Supper, and Last Couple Out. Both involved lots of running, something most children enjoy doing.

I remember playing Hide and Go Seek with my rural school students the first year I taught. That worked because the little schoolyard had bushes and trees. But the schoolyard where I attended as a child had neither, so I don't remember ever playing that game there.

I think the most important thing we used at recess those days was our imaginations. Maybe that's why we had so much fun.

Comic Strips in the Peach Section

One of the best things about being retired is having the leisure to read the entire newspaper while I sip my morning cup of coffee. I read pretty much everything in it, including the comics. In fact, I think they're about my favorite part of the paper.

Sometimes I think back to the comics of my childhood. My parents subscribed to the *Mitchell Daily Republic*, a daily printed in Mitchell, South Dakota, one of the big towns in our area. Every Saturday, that paper included the "peach section," a four-page spread of nothing but comics on peach-colored newsprint. Most of those strips are no longer being published, but I remember them vividly.

One of my favorites was *Boots and Her Buddies*. It featured a pretty young woman who always wore beautiful fashions. The best part was the last frame which had a paper doll of Boots and some pretty dresses to color, cut out, and play with.

I also liked *Mutt and Jeff*. Mutt was very tall and Jeff was very short. They always managed to get into humorous situations.

Then there was *Li'l Abner* with his family, the Yokums, who lived in Dogpatch, USA. For years, the beautiful Daisy Mae tried to get Li'l Abner to marry her, which he finally—reluctantly—did. That strip was filled with colorful characters, including pipe-smoking Mammy Yokum who tried to keep everyone under control.

Bringing Up Father told the humorous story of a newly rich Irish family. Jiggs, the father, longed to live as he had before becoming rich, while Maggie, his wife, tried to get him to climb the social ladder and live like rich people. I remember they had just blank circles for their eyes. *Little Orphan Annie* was depicted with that type of eyes, too.

I had a hard time getting into the story of the *Prince Valiant* comic strip, but I always looked at it because it was drawn so beautifully. It took up a full half of one page but nothing much seemed to happen.

Gasoline Alley was the first comic strip to allow its characters to age normally, eventually going on for a couple of generations. Walt Wallace was the first main character. Before he eventually married, he found a baby boy on his doorstep and raised him. The boy was named Skeezix, and he married and had children, which kept the strip going.

Some of the comics we enjoy today were already favorites when I was a child, such as *Blondie, Dick Tracy*, and *Beetle Bailey*. A few have story lines updated so they cover more contemporary situations.

I'm not sure if many papers put out entire comic sections anymore; maybe some bigger ones do. But I'd love to read a peach section again and revisit those old comic strip friends.

Growing Up With a Song in My Heart

I was fortunate to grow up in a family that loved music. Often we'd gather around the piano and sing hymns while Mama played. And she saw to it that all four of us children took piano lessons, for which I am thankful, even though I don't play well.

Daddy and his three brothers formed the Thum Brothers Quartet that sang for church services and lots of funerals. Whenever I hear the old hymn "Beyond the Sunset," I think of my dad and uncles who sang it so often. After my dad's oldest brother quit singing, my brother took his place to keep the group going for several more years.

Daddy learned to play the accordion when he was a teenager. He saved his money to buy his own instrument, an old-fashioned one with buttons instead of the keys used on newer models. He played for barn dances before he and my mom were married. In fact, they met at one of those old-fashioned events.

After they married and we children came along, Daddy no longer played for dances, but we often piled into the car and drove to Tyndall, South Dakota, a small town near our farm, to attend wedding dances. They were held in the city auditorium there.

There was always a live polka band playing on stage. People would pile their wedding gifts along the front of the stage, and that's where those gifts stayed until the dance was over.

Mama and we girls would sit in the balcony to watch the wedding party march in. Back then, most brides had their attendants wear pink or blue gowns. We were always excited to see when occasionally an adventuresome bride would have her attendants wear yellow or lilac.

The dancing started with the just the bride and groom dancing the first dance. I thought that looked so romantic.

Sometimes our family would drive to Groveland, a huge dance hall (at least it seemed huge to me when I was a girl) north of Tyndall. I never saw my parents dance there. Usually Mama and we girls sat in the car listening to the music and "people-watching" while Daddy and my brother mingled with friends outside.

I remember one night, a young couple in the car beside us started "making out." My younger sister wanted to watch them kissing, but she didn't want them to know she was watching. She put her sunglasses on to one side of her face so it would look as though she were looking straight ahead while she was actually watching the couple. I'm sure they never noticed!

I enjoyed watching my own children and now my grandchildren singing, playing piano, and joining band. I, too, continue my love of music by singing in our church choir. It's nice to know present generations of my family are continuing an interest in music that started with my own mom and dad years ago.

Pansies and Geraniums

Dolley Madison Quilt Block

That Old Golden Song Book

I imagine people who never attended rural school have a hard time figuring out how one teacher was able to teach every subject to eight grades every day. It kept everyone busy, that's for sure. But sometimes the entire school had a class together. Music was one of those whole-school classes.

Usually, we had music class just once a week, and we always looked forward to it. Most songs we sang were found in a paperback music book called *The Golden Book of Favorite Songs*. The cover was bright yellow, although most of those books in our school had long before lost their covers.

The pages were made of very thin paper. Many of our books had torn or even missing pages. We shared books when the song we wanted to sing was absent in a few of them.

I have a copy of that old music book. I can't remember where I got it. The cover and some pages are missing. The pages are yellowed around the edges, and some are torn. As I look through it, I remember many of the songs.

Christmas songs are all in one section. "Up on the Housetop" was one we all loved because we could go "ho, ho, ho" like Santa and "click, click, click" to make the sound of reindeer on the roof in the chorus of that song. We sang it at almost every school Christmas program.

All the traditional Christmas carols were included. We often sang those religious carols during our Christmas programs, too. Back then, we weren't worried about offending people who didn't believe in the religious side of Christmas.

Some old folk songs in that book would be considered "politically incorrect" now, too, I'm sure. For example, one was titled "Old Black Joe." It was a sentimental song which we enjoyed singing.

Other favorites of mine included "Darling Nellie Gray," "Juanita," "Susy, Little Susy," "Rueben and Rachel," and songs written by Stephen Foster. I was always curious about the song titled "Kathleen Mavourneen." We never sang it, maybe because we didn't know how to pronounce that last name!

Music class always ended with the favorite song of all of us—"The Farmer in the Dell." We loved it because of the actions which went along with it. One student would be the farmer. As the rest of us sang the first verse, that student walked around the room until he chose another student as the wife. Then, as we went on singing, that wife would choose the dog, the dog chose the cat, and so on.

My first year of teaching was in a small rural school near Scotland. I noticed when I entered the schoolroom the first day that there was no piano. I asked the school board if they would buy one for us. Much to my surprise and delight, they found a good secondhand piano and bought it for the school.

All my students were excited about having a piano in school. I even gave a few piano lessons to a couple of girls. I loved leading music class with my thirteen students. And we sang all the Christmas carols at the program we gave that year, just as when I was a student myself.

I noticed one can still buy copies of that wonderful *Golden Book of Favorite Songs* online, but I'm glad my copy looks well used. It reminds me of how much we loved all its wonderful old songs.

Daylilies

Author's childhood home showing driveway leading to the mail-box

The Mailbox at the End of the Driveway

Each day I check my e-mail first thing in the morning. I love getting and sending e-mail. It's such a fast and easy way of corresponding. But there are some things I miss about the way we sent and received mail when I was a child, when it all came to a box at the end of our driveway.

Our mailbox had the usual curved top we all remember and was mounted on a wooden fence post. In the summer, wild roses sometimes grew around the bottom of the post.

Daddy didn't paint our mailbox, so it was just the gray color of the metal from which it was made. On one side was a small metal flag, faded from its original red color, on a short metal pole. If we were mailing something, we'd put it in the mailbox before the rural mail carrier came, and then we'd raise the little metal flag to its upright position. That way, the mailman knew he had to take something out of the box before he put our mail into it.

We subscribed to a daily newspaper, which came one day after publication, so there was always mail six days a week. But I loved seeing envelopes in the mailbox, too. I don't remember ever getting "junk" mail, as we do these days. But we often had pen pals, sometimes as part of our curriculum in rural school.

I had a pen pal for several years in my early teens, but she wasn't one from school. I don't remember how we started corresponding. We were about the same age, but she was a whole lot more "worldly" than

I was. Maybe she just wasn't as shy as I was. Anyway, I loved reading about her boyfriends and up-to-date clothes.

Finding a package in the mailbox was always a source of excitement. Since my mother often ordered items from the many catalogs that also came in the mail, a package sometimes meant something new to wear. At Christmastime, it meant our toys had arrived. I'm sure my parents always hoped those packages arrived on school days, but I do remember seeing Daddy carrying a huge cardboard box from beside the mailbox down to his shop just before Christmas one year.

Daddy told us about the time he ordered an accordion all the way from Czechoslovakia when he was a young man. He ordered it though a catalog and waited anxiously for it to arrive. And it did—in a box the mailman dumped on the ground beside their mailbox. Fortunately, the accordion was still in perfect condition and was an important part of Daddy's life for many years.

When I use regular mail nowadays, I miss the prices we used to pay for postage. Stamps cost three cents, and the price never seemed to change. Postcards could be purchased and sent for one cent. But, even at those prices, we were careful to use them wisely.

I'd rather not have to depend on regular mail for all my correspondence these days, but I do miss that old mailbox, even though the surprise it held some days was just a spider weaving a web inside.

Irises

Author, left, with sisters, sister-in-law, and daughter
wearing slacks and stylish "big hair" at family
holiday event; author's niece and son in foreground

Women in Slacks—A New and Shocking Style

On these winter days, I appreciate wearing my warm slacks or heavy jeans. But women wearing slacks were not a common sight when I was a girl. Those days, women and girls were expected to wear dresses, no matter how cold it was. And our skirts were not very long, usually reaching just below the knee.

We girls often pulled on a pair of slacks under our skirts to go to school. If the schoolroom felt especially cold, we left them on all day. I remember we called it "Blaha Style" because the rural school I attended was named Blaha School.

We didn't wear short anklets with our dresses in winter, as we would in summer. No, in winter we had to wear dreaded cotton stockings. During the week, we wore tan stockings; on Sundays, we wore white stockings.

Those stocking came all the way up our legs and thighs and were held in place by garters attached to elastic garter belts worn around our waists. It seemed that no matter how much we pulled up those stockings before hooking on the garters, they always wrinkled around the knees after we sat down just once. Most of us hated wearing them.

Mama bought coveralls for us to wear as children, so we could play around the farm without skinning our knees. We could also wear slacks to pick cockleburs in the cornfields or shock oat bundles. But we had to wear dresses every time we went to town or church or visiting.

Mama wore cotton housedresses for everyday. She did all her work in them. That included not just housework, but also gardening, milking, and other outside work. I don't recall seeing her wear slacks until after I was married.

It wasn't until I was a young mother that it finally became acceptable for women to wear slacks. I remember the first Christmas when my sisters, nieces, and I all wore slacks to the family celebration. It was such a momentous occasion that we took a picture of us in our modern outfits!

About the same time, the local newspaper ran a photo of a nurse at Sacred Heart Hospital in Yankton wearing white slacks and a top to work. It was such a departure from their usual apparel that it made the front page of the paper.

I started my teaching career wearing dresses to school, even in rural school where I taught the first two years. When I started teaching in Yankton, dresses were still required. Finally, school officials relented and allowed us to wear slacks, but only as long as the top and bottom of the slacks outfit were of the same fabric. We would never have been allowed to wear jeans—not even on Fridays!

But at least I didn't have to struggle with long skirts the way my grandmothers and previous generations had to do. I can't imagine having a long skirt tangling around my ankles while chasing after a cow that had gotten into the cornfield.

I am thankful that slacks are now accepted as proper apparel for women, no matter what the occasion. Sure, it's fun to dress up in a skirt once in a while, but when the cold winter wind is blowing snowflakes around, I'll take warm slacks every time.

Misplaced Animals

Growing up on the farm, I always knew where each farm animal belonged, but they didn't always stay there. Animals not in their right places could be the cause of extra work—or a bit of enjoyment.

It was always a big chore getting cattle back in when they got out of the pasture fence. Sometimes we'd come home from town and find them in the cornfield. We had to get them out as fast as possible because they'd eat green corn until they got sick.

If we found them out on the road, it was a different situation. Sometimes Daddy would drive the car out to the cows farthest from home and start herding them back while we children were stationed along the road to keep them going in the right direction. We had to make sure they headed back to the opened gate in the pasture fence.

Sometimes our bull would go "visit" the neighbor's cows. It didn't take long before we'd get a phone call telling us we needed to get him home. That was a job for Daddy to handle.

If we had unusually deep snow, our cows could walk right over fences buried in drifts and wander away. That happened several times that I remember. I suppose Daddy kept them in the barn after we found them, at least until the snow melted a bit.

I don't remember pigs escaping their fence very often, but I'm sure they sometimes rooted their way out. And I do remember the little pigs Daddy called runts spending a few days in a cardboard box behind the cookstove in our kitchen. As soon as they seemed strong enough to rejoin their families out in the hog shed, they'd be gone. But we children enjoyed a few days playing with them.

Every late spring, we children had to help our parents catch the young hens, called pullets, and carry them to the hen house so they'd get used to being there, instead of all over the yard, before they started laying eggs. We had a long stick with a wire hook at the end to get them out of trees where some of them roosted. By the time we had them in the hen house, we were hot, sweaty, tired, and a bit scratched up.

Mama always complained when chickens found their way up to the front steps of the house. They made a big mess right in front of the door. She was really happy when Daddy finally put up a fence around the house.

While most of our cats were barn cats, Mama had her two favorites that enjoyed snoozing under the cookstove. We children brought kittens into the house once in a while, too, but mostly we played with them in the barn.

Of course, we human "animals" didn't always stay where we should when we were children either. Sometimes when Mama and Daddy went to town and left us home alone in the summertime, we'd go "swimming" in the stock tank. We didn't seem to mind the mossy bottom or the fact that cows had slurped in the water. I don't think we ever got caught, but I suppose our parents suspected what we'd been doing.

When I think of all the problems we faced with our animals, I guess I'm glad they're all in place now—in my memory.

Beware the Regal Rooster

He portrayed himself as The Farmyard King
And sported a floppy red crown to prove it.
His reddish brown wing feathers gleamed,
And his arching tail plumes flashed
Shades of purple and green in the summer sunshine.
He strutted about on scaly yellow feet
With purposeful staccato steps,
Head snapping this way and that,
Wattle flipping, eyes alert.
He knew his responsibilities.
He roused the farmer at sunrise each day
With his loud and raucous crow.
He supervised his harem of contented hens,
And bristled at the farmer's wife
When she came to the hen house with pails of oats.
But this cocky bird's favorite job, I'm convinced,
Was chasing me whenever he had the chance,
His talons threatening scratches on my legs.
He seemed to take great pleasure in
Scaring the living daylights
Out of a child like me.

Petunia Duet

Washing Dishes

The first thing my son and daughter wanted me to buy after I resumed my teaching career was a dishwasher. They both hated that chore when they were young. I knew how they felt because I had hated it as a child, too. But I think I had more reasons to dislike it; it was a whole lot more work back then.

Those were the days before we had electricity or running water. So, the first thing we had to do when dishes needed washing was heat some water. Usually by the time Mama had made a meal on the cook-stove, there was a big teakettle full of hot water ready to use.

After each meal, the dishes had to be scraped and stacked on one side of the kitchen table. My sisters and I, of course, had a rule about that: the dish washer stacks the dishes. Later, the dish wiper would put them away.

Next, the dish washer had to fill a big dishpan with hot water and add soap. A second pan was filled with hot water for rinsing the dishes.

We didn't let the dishes air dry; we wiped them. It usually took more than one towel (made from flour sacks) to dry all the dishes for our family of six.

We had a second rule about the job: what the dish washer misses, the wiper has to rinse off. That makes me wonder how clean the rinse water was by the time we finished this chore.

After all the dishes were washed and the oilcloth covering the table wiped clean, the pans of water had to be emptied outside. Then we traded washing/wiping jobs after the next meal.

I remember how excited we were when we finally had running water in the house. That's when Mama had Daddy put in a double sink, something she had dreamed of having. We could wash and rinse dishes more easily in the sinks. But it still wasn't any fun.

Mama really loved her new sinks. She made us wipe them dry each time we used them.

One day when I was reaching for something in the cupboards over the sink, I accidentally knocked over the big bottle of Watkins vanilla. It fell into one of the sinks, making a little chip in it. I dreaded telling Mama what I had done to her wonderful sink. Apparently she realized how terrible I felt about it because she didn't scold me. I still remember how relieved I was.

Getting a dishwasher was a big deal for my own children, and I appreciated it, too. But there was still a job that neither my children nor I liked doing—unloading the darn thing.

Red Onions

Monkey Wrench Quilt Block

Daddy Was a Farmer and a Barber

My dad was a farmer, but that's not what he had wanted to be as he grew up. He wanted to be a barber.

He taught himself how to cut men's hair and began trimming hair for many of the neighbors while he was still in his teens. But he really longed to go to trade school so he could cut hair in a shop in town. When his mother mentioned that to a neighbor lady, she declared, "Oh, don't let him be a barber. All barbers die of consumption." ("Consumption" was the common term for tuberculosis at that time.) So Daddy never did get to go to barber school, but he cut hair for men most of his life.

As a young man, Daddy used the money he earned cutting hair so he and his brother could buy an accordion. He learned to play it and often did so at dances in homes. He enjoyed seeing couples swirl around the kitchen to his polkas and waltzes. He met my mother at one of those dances.

Mama and Daddy were married in the "Dirty Thirties." They rented a farm and began the struggle of trying to make a living. They raked thistles to feed their cows instead of going on a honeymoon. Daddy decided he'd have to continue cutting hair to make ends meet. He bought a secondhand barber chair and set it up in a corner of the big farmhouse kitchen. Back in those days, there weren't laws prohibiting such things.

Each evening, after a long, hard day in the fields, Daddy would cut hair. Chairs were set up around the kitchen for those waiting their turn. Since the "customers" were all friends or relatives, this became a social event. Sometimes entire families came along.

Of course, when you had company, you were expected to serve them refreshments before they went home. Almost every day, Mama baked a cake or cookies. I remember she complained that she just couldn't bake a good white cake, so most often she served a rich sour cream chocolate cake or a dependable yellow cake.

Daddy charged twenty-five cents for each haircut. For their quarter, the men got not just a haircut, but also an evening's visiting and a cup of coffee and dessert. That was quite a bargain! But my parents knew they made good money from the haircuts. Sometimes, however, they wished people wouldn't stay so long after their haircuts and snacks were done.

When my parents retired to town, Daddy set up his barber chair in the basement of their house. He no longer cut hair except for his grandchildren now and then. However, I married a barber, and he gave Daddy haircuts while he sat in the same chair his customers had used for so many years.

A few years after Daddy died, Mama decided to sell out and move into an apartment. Daddy's barber chair had to be sold. My brother and I bought it and donated it to the museum in my parents' hometown (Scotland, South Dakota). It's a reminder of my dad, who got his wish to be a barber, even without formal training. And he never did come down with "consumption."

The Big Iron Cookstove in the Kitchen

It's so easy to feel warm and cozy these days as winter winds blow around our well-insulated houses. All we have to do is move a tiny dial on the thermostat, and we're as warm as we want to be. Perhaps we'd be a bit more thankful for that "instant warmth" if we thought for a few moments about the days when the heat in our homes came partly from our own exertions and never did reach the corners of rooms.

The farmhouse in which I grew up had two sources of heat—the big iron stove in the kitchen and a kerosene burner in the dining room. Heat from the kitchen stove wafted up through a register in the ceiling to warm the bedroom over the kitchen where we children slept.

The kerosene burner in the dining room wasn't used unless we were expecting company, so I'm sure our parents' bedroom over the dining room was often downright cold during long winter nights. No wonder we all used down-filled mattresses and covered up with thick woolen blankets.

Many of the best memories of my childhood home center on that iron cookstove sitting at one side of the big, square, farmhouse kitchen. Mama kept its pale green enameled sides and black cooktop spotless and gleaming. The reservoir on one end had become rusty, so we didn't use it to heat water for cooking, but there was always water in it. Attached to the top of the metal sheet extending upward from the back of the cooktop was a warming shelf, the perfect place for storing

97

crackers to keep them crisp. It also held a pile of hot pads and a set of large green glass salt and pepper shakers with dented tin tops.

We burned dry corncobs in the stove most of the time, and keeping the cob box filled was a job for us children. Every day after school, out we'd go, bundled up in flannel shawls over our heads, warm coats, and heavy gloves. After we'd filled the galvanized tub to the top, we'd stick in a row of cobs upright around the rim so we could add another four or five inches of cobs. By the time we were done, we'd be a bit warmer already.

Warmth radiated from the cookstove, doing a pretty good job of heating the entire kitchen, but it was always warmest right next to it. Sometimes in the morning before the stove could even begin to heat the kitchen, Mama would allow us to open the oven door and lean on it to get thawed out after coming in from milking the cows.

I can still smell the soups simmering at the back of the stove on cold winter days, and Mama's fried chicken that would have to be cooked near the front of the stove where the fire made the surface the hottest. Mama was able to regulate the stove's output of heat by adjusting a damper in the pipe leading from it to the chimney. She could even get the temperature right to bake cookies, cakes, and bread in the oven.

Mama and Daddy eventually added a three-burner kerosene stove in the kitchen. After we got electricity, an electric stove in the kitchen and gas furnace in the basement replaced the old iron stove. But whether it was bathing on Saturday nights with the tub sitting right beside the stove or pulling the kitchen table a little closer to it to play board games, those wonderful cozy times of a family together in a kitchen heated by a big old stove still warm my memories.

Beets

Antique Christmas ornament -
treasured remembrance of the author's mother

Old Treasures

I'm not one to keep things I don't use. I call myself "a thrower, not a keeper." But I have to admit I have sentimental attachments to some items and keep putting them back in drawers or on shelves in the basement, even when I'm in a cleaning mood.

One such item is a dented aluminum roaster with lots of black grease burned into crevices on the bottom. It belonged to my beloved mother-in-law and brings back memories of many happy meals eaten at her house with the extended family. I never look at that roaster without remembering the day she told me about a neighborhood family her family used to visit when she was a girl. Sometimes they ate with that family, and, if there were a kettle with food cooked onto it, the lady of that house would put it into the slop pail—a pail where people dumped water from the basin in which they washed their hands—to let it soak. I would tease my mother-in-law about putting that aluminum roaster in the slop pail when we were doing dishes. Of course she never would have done that; she didn't even have a slop pail in her kitchen.

I also hold on to my mom's food grinder. I used it quite a bit in my home until I got my food processor. That new tool does the same work much more easily than cranking the old food grinder. But I won't give it away. It brings back happy memories of helping Mama make delicious food like the gelatin salad with peaches, pineapple, and ground carrots.

My collection of Christmas ornaments includes one Mama gave me years ago. She received it from her grandma who likely brought it to

101

this country when emigrating from Russia in the 1870s, so it's official-
ly an antique. It's a small "chime" that has three candles around the
bottom. When the candles were lit, the rising heat made a metal circle
above them rotate, causing small metal rods hanging from it to strike
bells below. Attached to the center rod is a tin circle with the nativity
scene on it and the words "Glory to God in Heaven; Peace on Earth,
Goodwill to Men" written in German. Some parts are missing, but I
put it out every Christmas, just to remember Mama.

I have a box of beautiful handkerchiefs I received in my early years
of teaching. They're really too delicate and lovely to use. I've always
hoped to find a way to show them off, but, so far, I haven't thought of
one. I just have to keep them, in case I ever do.

Tucked away in the drawer of my hutch are several small candles
in Thanksgiving and Halloween shapes. I bought them when I was just
a bride, and that's getting close to sixty years ago. I never lit them, so
they're almost as good as new—if you don't look at the tiny scratches in the wax. They have so many memories attached that I just can't
throw them away.

When I stop to think about it, I guess there are quite a few things in
my house that I keep because of the memories associated with them or
in honor of those who gave them to me. Hmmm. I wonder if anyone
will ever want all those letters my husband sent me when he was in the
Army before we were even engaged. Should I throw them out? Well . . .
maybe not this year.

Sunday School in a Rural Church

The first church I attended as a child was small, one-room, rural, and about a mile from our farm. Almost everyone who attended was a relative of mine. That made Sunday morning a special time for the family.

The adults followed a tradition of having women sit on one side of the center aisle and men on the other. I remember when a young woman who had attended the church during her growing-up years returned with her fiancé and sat with him on the "men's side." Everyone stared in shock. But her brave action didn't inspire any of the other women to follow suit.

Sunday School was conducted during the first hour. We children all sat at the front on the "women's" side. Our moms, some of them holding baby siblings, sat behind us. The men visited outside until Sunday School was over. All except one man—the Sunday School teacher. He had to be inside, trying to get us to pay attention as he read aloud our lesson.

At the end of the lesson, we recited a Bible verse printed on a little card with a picture to illustrate the verse. If we recited it properly, we were allowed to keep the card. When we had a certain number of little cards, we could trade them in for a larger, postcard-sized card. I wonder what ever happened to all those cards since neither my siblings nor I have any now.

Our pastor served four rural churches so he came to us only once a month. Women of the church vied for the privilege of inviting him and his family for Sunday dinner. I loved it when Mama was successful in having them come to our house. The pastor and his wife had two children about my age to play with after the meal.

On the Sundays when the pastor was at other churches, one of the older men read a sermon from a big brown book—in high German. Of course we children couldn't understand a word of it, so we often became restless.

One Sunday, we must have been naughtier than usual because, after the German sermon, the reader told us the story of Jesus in the Temple when he was a boy and suggested we should use that as our model of behavior in church.

After the service was over, the men again gathered outdoors—in cars, during winter—while the women stood around the small entryway and visited. It was a time for catching up on family news. If a family was absent, the women were sure to find out why.

Most people made it a point to attend services every Sunday. It wasn't just their piety calling them; it was a social occasion for those who spent most of the week with just their immediate families. That made church the place to be on Sunday morning.

How Did Mama Manage on Washday?

If you're like me, you often wish your parents were around to answer questions you should have asked when they still were. I'd ask my mom how she ever managed washdays when we were children. For one thing, Mama often had two children in diapers at a time because my siblings and I are all just two years apart in age. And, in those days, no one had ever heard of disposable diapers, so she obviously had a lot of laundry to do.

For another thing, Mama's washing machine was in a building a few yards from the house. It was a building with three sections. One was used for storage, one as a garage for various farm machines or the car, and one was where the washing machine, cream separator, cob-burning cookstove, and an old table almost filled the space.

Washday, which was always Monday, would have started with Mama getting a good fire going in the cookstove in that building. Then she had to carry water from the cistern near the house to fill a big copper tub on the stove. After the water was scalding hot, she had to transfer it, one kettleful at a time, into the wringer washer.

Washing with that type of machine took hours. That makes me wonder what Mama did with four little children, one a baby, while she washed clothes. I suppose Daddy could watch us sometimes, especially in winter when he didn't have fieldwork. But, even then, there would have been days he wouldn't have had time.

I wonder if Mama transported all four of us down to the washhouse with her some days. That would have been quite a hassle, especially in the wintertime. Or did she find a way to be sure we were safe, alone in the house? If she did that, I imagine she had to make many a quick trip back to the house to check on us.

I don't think Mama had a hired girl to help out when we were very young. I remember we had them later, after Mama had to have major surgery which required a long recovery. We children usually liked the girls, but I remember one named Helen who apparently didn't like us any more than we liked her.

I recall one day as Helen worked in the kitchen, we children went upstairs to our bedroom directly above. We looked through the heat register in the bedroom floor and watched Helen working below us. Then one of us—and I'll never tell who—decided to spit down through the register onto Helen. We all ended up in trouble over that little escapade.

My dear mother worked hard every day on the farm, but I'm sure laundry day was one of the busiest and hardest to manage. I wish I could ask her about it.

How Thanksgiving Used to Look

As I contemplate our plans for Thanksgiving each year, my mind wanders back to the way we celebrated it when I was a child. It occurs to me that our big, noisy, family Thanksgivings way back then were quite different from our quiet little gatherings these days. They even looked different.

For one thing, our gatherings used to consist of three generations—grandparents, aunts and uncles, and lots of cousins. Nowadays, with families so scattered, our group consists of only adults in just two generations.

The setting was different, too. My mother's parents lived in a huge old house about a block off Main Street in Tripp, South Dakota. The kitchen wasn't very big, so it was crowded as all the aunts helped Grandma cook the meal, but they had a lot of fun, talking and laughing.

Grandpa and my dad and uncles sat in the formal parlor while waiting for the meal, which, by the way, was served to them before anyone else. That parlor featured big chairs all around the perimeter and lots of smoke from Grandpa's cigars and a few cigarette smokers.

I can still see the lace curtains at the bay windows in the dining room. The table had been expanded to be as large as all available leaves could make it and was covered with a white linen cloth. Along one wall was a buffet; sitting on it was one of those old-fashioned mantel clocks with a round top. It announced the hours with a metallic-sounding chime.

Things were just a bit different at my paternal grandma's house in Scotland. The kitchen was small there, too, but there weren't quite as many aunts on that side of my family, so it wasn't as crowded as at the other grandma's.

The dining room also featured lace curtains at a bay window. That grandma's table nearly filled the room when extended with its nine leaves. Along one side of the room stood Grandma's sewing machine. A curio cabinet jam-packed with delicate knickknacks dominated one corner.

The men there sat in the parlor, too, while waiting to be served. But that grandma's parlor was quite small. An overstuffed, brown, plush-covered couch with matching chair pretty much filled it.

So where were we children as the adults prepared for the feast? Well, at the house in Tripp, we were sent down into the basement to play because we were pretty noisy, being that there were over twenty of us. After the meal, we usually all trooped downtown, older cousins holding hands of younger ones, where we attended a movie. That gave the adults some peace and quiet to enjoy an afternoon of visiting.

There weren't as many cousins on my dad's side, so we usually entertained ourselves without getting too much in the way.

Absent in those mental pictures from the past are items we take so much for granted today: televisions blaring footballs games, cell phones with users texting others while ignoring those next to them, microwave ovens to defrost and cook ready-made foods, and female relatives wearing slacks instead of dresses. Well, I can live without most of those things, but I do prefer slacks on cold winter days!

I have many memories of those Thanksgivings so long ago, but that's not all I have. When my grandma in Scotland passed away, I bought her big dining room table with its nine leaves. It's still in my basement where I sometimes hosted big gatherings of people for holidays. I don't do that anymore, but I never pass that beautiful old round table without seeing again in my mind those wonderful Thanksgivings of long ago.

Carrots

Nine Patch Quilt Block

YCL Tried to Make Us Better Citizens

Years ago, most South Dakota rural schools had a chapter of the Young Citizens League. It was started here in 1910 and went on as a state organization until 1971. The purpose was to develop character, citizenship, and individual responsibility in students.

I remember belonging to YCL in the rural school I attended. It was sort of like a club. We'd have meetings regularly—I think about once a month—and elect officers. But, mostly, it seemed to be a way to get us students to help clean the schoolroom and keep the schoolyard neat.

A list of duties was discussed at each meeting, and children volunteered or were appointed to do them. Bigger children had to sweep the classroom floor each day and bring in a pail of water from the cistern each morning. Little children did jobs such as emptying wastebaskets, "clapping" blackboard erasers outdoors to get the chalk dust out of them, and picking up trash on the playground.

One of my favorite jobs was clapping the erasers. Maybe it helped get out any frustrations I had. I hated sweeping the floor when I got older because all "duties" had to be done during last recess, and sweeping the classroom took most of the recess time.

Once a month, the job of sweeping was especially messy. That was when the teacher spread sweeping compound over the wooden floors to clean them and help remove dust. Sweeping compound consisted of sawdust soaked in oil. It made the floors look pink.

The teacher would spread the compound over the floor in the morning so we could walk it into the floor all day. That was also the day we were allowed to play Fruit Basket Upset during recess. That game, a favorite of all of us, involved lots of running. It really helped grind the compound into the floor.

Another part of YCL was encouraging health and cleanliness. The teacher would check to see if our fingernails were clean each morning and ask if we'd brushed our teeth. If we passed the examination, we'd receive a little sticker to put on a chart. I seem to remember the stickers were pictures of tiny bars of Ivory soap.

I enjoyed the YCL monthly meetings because they took a big chunk out of one afternoon of class time. We followed Robert's Rules of Order and all learned how to conduct a meeting. That's a skill I use to this day.

I remember receiving little round pins occasionally that had something to do with YCL. I suppose they were awards for achievements relating to the organization. I wish I would have kept those pins, but, like so many things from the past, they are now just part of a happy memory.

Forsythia

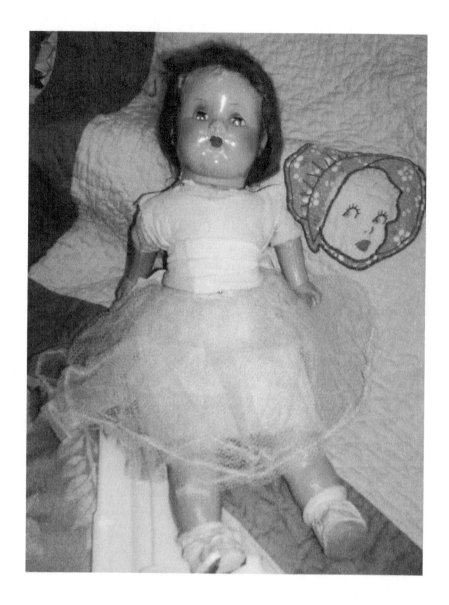

Author's childhood doll

Christmas Catalogs

Do they still print those big fat catalogs they used to send out in the mail years ago? They were so thick you could put two or three of them on a chair to raise a small child to the proper level to eat off the big people's table.

How we looked forward to new catalogs every spring and fall. We'd pore over the pages, seeing beautiful dresses and shoes we could only dream about ordering. Usually, we'd show Mama the dress we liked best, and she'd sew us one that looked pretty much like it—but only if we needed a new dress.

When a new catalog arrived, we'd have permission to use the old one to cut out dresses for our paper dolls. Of course, they never fit the dolls exactly right, but we didn't care. We thought our paper dolls looked beautiful in their new dresses anyway.

The best catalogs were those that arrived early in November—the annual Christmas toy catalogs! We almost wore them out long before Christmas came. They showed toys we hardly ever see in ads nowadays. No video games, no bratty dolls, nothing that needed a battery.

Instead, the boys found train sets and toy tractors and little cars. They decided which cowboy holster and gun set looked the fanciest. They longed for Tinkertoys and building block sets and miniature tools just like their dads used.

And we girls went directly to the doll section. We loved cute baby dolls with real-looking baby bottles. We studied the pages of little girl dolls to be sure we'd selected the one with the prettiest dress. And we spent hours staring at bride dolls, although we never really wanted one of them. They were mostly to put on a shelf; we wanted to play with our dolls.

We didn't expect a new doll every Christmas. My sisters and I each had a nice doll with bisque face, arms, and legs. Their stuffed fabric bodies were comfortable to cuddle. They had fuzzy hair made from some kind of synthetic fibers. I still have mine, wrapped in a small quilt my grandma made for it when I was a girl. It's one of my childhood treasures.

We girls also enjoyed catalog pages showing little kitchen sets and dishes. Apparently being a wife and mother was the goal of many little girls back then, since most of the toys offered to them were of a domestic nature.

We were sure to show Mama exactly which toys we liked best in the Christmas catalog. We didn't expect more than one or two to show up on Christmas morning. We knew we'd also be getting needed clothing. Maybe that's why we treasured so much the few toys we did receive.

I feel sorry for today's children who are bombarded constantly, starting before Halloween, with ads for spectacular toys on television, and who eventually find a whole stack of them under their Christmas trees. Many leave nothing for them to do with their own imaginations.

Like the girls in the Laura Ingalls Wilder books, who were thrilled with their meager Christmas gifts, we appreciated what we received mainly because we weren't overwhelmed with the abundance of our gifts—just with the abundance of love with which they were given.

Delicious Christmas Treats

Christmastime brings back so many wonderful childhood memories: the excitement of rural school programs, loud and loving family gatherings, candles and carols at Christmas Eve church services, and treats we enjoyed only at that magical time of year.

Mama's egg money didn't stretch far enough most weeks to buy anything beyond necessary staples on our Saturday night trip to town. But, somehow, as Christmas drew near, she found money to buy extra sugar and other ingredients to make holiday treats.

I loved Mama's homemade caramels, made with our own sweet cream. Mama added chocolate to half the batch. Those were my favorites.

Our holiday popcorn balls started with a brown sugar syrup Mama made, and lots of popped corn. After Mama poured the hot syrup over the popcorn, we'd butter our fingers and form the mixture into big balls as quickly as we could. Then we'd wrap them in wax paper and hope we could sample them long before Christmas Day.

One of our neighbors always ordered big boxes of chocolates which he sold in smaller quantities to families in the neighborhood. Mama bought chocolate stars, chocolate-covered raisins, and big clusters of chocolate-covered peanuts.

And she always bought a particular candy that consisted of a small mound of firm, white, very sweet, vanilla-flavored filling covered in a thin coating of milk chocolate. She called those candies "Haughties" because they reminded her of a brown-and-white cow we had named "Haughty."

Mama also managed to find enough money to buy hard-shelled nuts, apples, oranges, figs, and dates to eat during the holidays. I especially loved the honey brown figs pressed flat into a small rectangular box wrapped in cellophane. Each luscious bite was filled with sweet, crunchy seeds.

We children always looked forward to the Christmas sacks we'd receive after rural school and church programs. They were filled with nuts, fruit, and candy, including those wonderful little hard candies that looked like pieces of curly Christmas ribbon.

Another hard candy I loved looked as though it had been sliced off a roll. In the center of each piece was the picture of a tiny flower, complete with stem and leaves. I always wondered how they got those designs in that candy.

I can still picture our family, sitting around the kitchen table laden with holiday treats, often joined by relatives who'd stopped for a visit. I remember Mama would choose an apple or orange or use the nutcracker to eat hard-shelled nuts, while we children reached for candy and popcorn balls. Only now that I'm a grown-up do I suspect she chose the fruit or nuts so we children could have more candy because it was a rare treat. And that's just another sweet Christmas memory.

The Forgotten Promise

B rittle December sunshine streamed in through the west windows of my small one-room schoolhouse that afternoon, many years ago, as I graded papers and then cleared my desk. I shut down the oil heater in the center of the room and slipped into my coat. "Hurry, Donna," I whispered to myself, as I stood by the window watching for my younger sister who picked me up every day on her way home from high school.

Though I was only nineteen years old, with just one year of college training, and still lived with my parents on their farm, I felt independent and quite grown-up. I was a certified teacher, after all, and this room was the tiny world where I was in charge of everything.

I smiled as I thought about how excited my former college roommate, Joanie, must feel right then. She was a "one-year wonder," too, teaching in the nearby rural school I had attended as a child, and that evening her students would present their Christmas program. I couldn't be late for her special night.

At last I saw my sister coming down the road. I reached into my pocket and pulled out my gloves. A piece of paper fluttered to the floor. I picked it up and recognized my own handwriting.

"Oh, no!" I groaned as I read the words: "Remember to make three pies for the lunch at Joanie's Christmas program."

I had forgotten all about the note, and it was too late now to make pies. I felt my cheeks redden with humiliation. What would I say to

Joanie? All the smug self-confidence I had felt just minutes ago faded as I climbed into the car.

Mama was putting fried chicken on the supper table as my sister and I came into the kitchen. Suddenly, I stopped and gasped. On the counter were three beautiful apple pies.

"Mama!" I cried. "I didn't tell you I'd promised to bring three pies tonight. How did you know?"

"Oh, I always take pies to the Christmas program at our school," said Mama. "Sit down, girls. Supper's ready."

For a moment, I just stood there, letting my mother's calm efficiency restore my self-confidence, now tempered with a good dose of modesty. Then I said, "Thank you, Mama." And I didn't feel too grown-up to give her a quick hug.

Acknowledgements

Thanks to Loretta Sorensen, without whose expertise in publishing I would not have had the courage to tackle this project; to my niece Melanie Bender for designing the perfect cover; to Kathy Grow for her careful editing; and to my longtime friend Beverly Behrens for providing the lovely watercolor paintings that add so much to the book. And, as always, thanks to my husband, Bud, for his love, support, and encouragement.
MK

I thank Marilyn, my dear friend since that first year at college, for her charm and inspiration— warm and bright as the quilts and gardens we both cherish. I am forever grateful for the support of my dear husband Ralph and for his helpful comments as well as his expertise with digital aspects of producing art these days.
BB

CPSIA information can be obtained
at www.ICGtesting.com
Printed in the USA
FSOW03n1827280815
10453FS